A Book of Simple Living

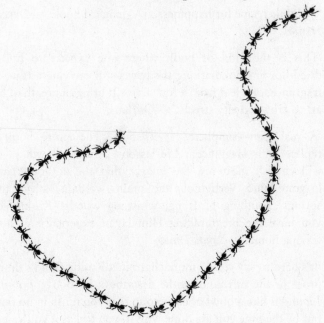

'A simple recipe for happiness...[A] magical book.' —*Deccan Herald*

'This is the kind of book where one expects to find a dried flower bookmarking the pages still carrying a trace of fragrance, or a leaf from a lime tree...It brings a breath of hill air to crowded city streets.' —*Outlook*

'A real gem—simplicity at its best...The entire book is replete with magnificent life lessons. Above all, what you will cherish most are the images that the author creates in your mind. Vertiginous mountains, verdant valleys, tiny springs...soothing birdsong, whistling woods—Ruskin lets you have the breathtaking Himalayan experience without leaving home.' —*Sakal Times*

'It's hard to say what's more charming, Ruskin Bond's simple prose or the surroundings he describes...[*A Book of Simple Living*] is like a bowl of clear soup that you finish in no time, but by the time you are done with it, you feel as if you've had a five-course meal.' —*The Hindu*

'In gnomic pieces reminiscent of the short and evocative poems of old Buddhist Chinese poets like Wang Wei, Bond muses about nature, change, the life of the mind and the pleasures of the flesh...This beautifully produced slim volume is perfect for random dippings. Even now, so many people know Bond only as a writer of children's stories, like the Rusty books. *Simple Living* makes one realise just how much more there is to him, and how much we will miss him when Rusty does finally run away.' —*Outlook Traveller*

A Book of Simple Living

Brief Notes from the Hills

RUSKIN BOND

SPEAKING
TIGER

SPEAKING TIGER BOOKS LLP.
4381/4, Ansari Road, Daryaganj
New Delhi-110002, India

Copyright © Ruskin Bond 2015

First published in Speaking Tiger as a hardback in 2015

ISBN: 978-81-930710-0-7

10 9 8 7 6

The moral right of the author has been asserted.

Typeset in Goudy Old Style by SÜRYA, New Delhi
Printed at Chaman Enterprises, New Delhi

In the name of God, stop a moment, cease your work, look around you.

—Leo Tolstoy

After all, it is a good thing to laugh...and if a straw can tickle a man, it is an instrument of happiness.

—John Dryden

Introduction

What have I learnt after eighty years on planet earth? Quite frankly, very little. Dear reader, don't believe the elders and philosophers. Wisdom does not come with age. Maybe it is born in the cradle—but this too is conjecture. I only know that for the most part I have followed instinct rather than intelligence, and this has resulted in a modicum of happiness. You will find your own way to this reward, which is in the end the only reward worth having. All that this book can do is to show you that there was a fellow traveller.

To have got to this point in life without the solace of religion says something for all the things that have brought me joy and a degree of contentment. Books, of course; I couldn't have survived without books and stories. And companionship—which is sometimes friendship, sometimes love and sometimes, if we are lucky, both. And a little light laughter, a sense of humour. And, above all, my relationship with the natural world—up here in the hills; in the dusty plains; in a treeless mohalla choked with concrete flats, where I once found a marigold growing out of a crack in a balcony. I removed the plaster from the base of the plant, and filled in a little earth which I watered every morning. The plant grew, and sometimes it produced a little orange flower, which I plucked and gave away before it died.

This much I can tell you: for all its hardships and complications, life is simple. And a nature that doesn't sue for happiness often receives it in large measure.

Was it accidental, or was it ordained, or was it in my nature to arrive unharmed at this final stage of life's journey? I love this life passionately, and I wish it could go on and on. But all good things must come to an end, and when the time comes to make my exit, I hope I can do so with good grace and humour.

But there is time yet, and many small moments to savour.

Landour, Mussoorie　　　　　　　　　RUSKIN BOND
New Year's Day, 2015

A small ginger cat arrives on my terrace every afternoon, to curl up in the sun and slumber peacefully for a couple of hours.

When he awakes, he gets on his feet with minimum effort, arches his back and walks away as he had come. The same spot every day, the same posture, the same pace. There may be better spots—sunnier, quieter, frequented by birds that can be hunted when the cat is rested and restored. But there is no guarantee, and the search will be never-ending, and there may rarely be time to sleep after all that searching and finding.

It occurs to me that perhaps the cat is a monk. By this I do not mean anything austere. I doubt anyone in single-minded pursuit of enlightenment ever finds it. A good monk would be a mild sort of fellow, a bit of a sensualist, capable of compassion for the world, but also for himself. He would know that it is all right not to climb every mountain.

A good monk would know that contentment is easier to attain than happiness, and that it is enough.

—

And what of happiness, then?

Happiness is a mysterious thing, to be found somewhere between too little and too much. But it is as elusive as a butterfly, and we must never pursue it. If we stay very still, it may come and settle on our hand. But only briefly. We must savour those moments, for they will not come our way very often.

A cherry tree bowed down by the night's rain suddenly rights itself, flinging pellets of water in my face. This, too, is happiness.

———

Mist fills the Himalayan valleys, and monsoon rain sweeps across the hills. Sometimes, during the day, a bird visits me—a deep purple whistling thrush, hopping about on long dainty legs, peering to right and left, too nervous to sing. She perches on the window sill, and looks out with me at the rain. She does not permit any familiarity. But if I sit quietly in my chair, she will sit quietly on her window sill, glancing quickly at me now and then just to make sure that I'm keeping my distance. When the rain stops, she glides away, and it is only then, confident in her freedom, that she bursts into full-throated song, her broken but haunting melody echoing down the ravine.

A squirrel comes, too, when his home in the oak tree gets waterlogged. Apparently he is a bachelor; anyway, he lives alone. He knows me well, this squirrel, and is bold enough to climb on to the dining table looking for tidbits, which he always finds, because I leave them there. Had I met him when he was a youngster, he would have learned to eat from my hand, but I have only been in this house a few months. I like it this way. I'm not looking for pets; it is enough that he seeks me out when he wants company.

A cold, cold January. There is a blizzard. The storm rages for two days—howling winds, hail, sleet, snow. The power goes out. There's coal to burn but it is hardly enough. Worst weather that I can recall in this hill station. Sick of it. Why do I stay here?

In March, there's gentle weather at last. Peach, plum and apricot trees in blossom, birds making a racket in the branches. So this is why I stay.

—

As I walked home last night,
I saw a lone fox dancing
In the cold moonlight.

I stood and watched; then
Took the low road, knowing
The night was his by right.

Sometimes, when words ring true,
I'm like a lone fox dancing
In the morning dew.

The leaves are a fresh pale green in the spring rain. I can look at the trees from my window—look down on them almost, because the window is on the first floor of the cottage, and the hillside runs at a sharp angle into the ravine. I do nearly all my writing at this window seat. Whenever I look up, the trees remind me that they are there. They are my best critics. As long as I am aware of their presence, I may avoid the thoughtless and the trivial.

In the days when I walked a lot I went among the trees on my hillside often, acknowledging their presence with a touch of my hand against their trunks—the walnut's smooth and polished; the pine's patterned and whorled; the oak's rough and gnarled, full of experience. The oak had been there the longest, and the wind had bent its upper branches and twisted a few, so that it looked shaggy and undistinguished. It was a good tree for the privacy of birds, its crooked branches spreading out with no particular effect; and sometimes the tree seemed uninhabited until there was a whirring sound, as of a helicopter approaching, and a party of long-tailed blue magpies shot out of the leaves and streamed across the forest glade.

After the monsoon, when the dark red berries had ripened on the hawthorn, this pretty tree was visited by green pigeons, the kokla birds of Garhwal, who clambered upside-down among the fruit-laden twigs. And during winter, a white-capped redstart perched on the bare branches of the wild pear tree and whistled cheerfully. He had come to winter in the garden.

The pines grew on the next hill. But there was a small blue one, a Himalayan chir, a little way below my cottage, and sometimes I sat beneath it to listen to the wind playing softly in its branches.

Opening the window at night, I usually had something else to listen to—the mellow whistle of the pygmy owlet, or the cry of a barking deer which had scented the proximity of a panther.

Some sounds I could not recognize at the time. They were strange night sounds that I now know as the sounds of the great trees themselves, scratching their limbs in the dark, shifting a little, flexing their fingers.

Sometimes, there would be a strange silence, and I would see the moon coming up, and two distant deodars in perfect silhouette.

—

In bed with fever. Beside my bed is a window and I like looking out at all that's happening around me; it distracts me from the aches and pains.

The cherry leaves are turning a dark green. On the maple tree, winged seeds spin round and round. There is fruit on the wild blackberry bushes. Two mynah birds are building a nest in a hole in the wall above the window. They're very noisy about it, quarelling like good married people; bits of grass keep falling on the window sill. High up the spruce tree, a hawk cuckoo calls: 'I slept so well! I slept so well!' (And so did I, happy bird, despite the fever!) A small squirrel climbs on the window sill. He's been coming every day since I've been ill, and I give him crumbs from my plate. A boy on a mule passes by on the rough mountain track. He sees my face at the window and waves to me. I wave back to him. When I'm better, I'll ask him to let me ride his mule.

Winter is here again. When it gets dark I take my place by the large stove in the little dining room. Rakesh sits with me, his wife Beena is making comforting music in the kitchen, frying and stirring masalas in the kadhai. Their children, Siddharth, Shrishti and Gautam, are making a racket in the room above us. The little cat has curled itself into a ball next to my chair.

This is my family, and it began with friendship, with Prem Singh, Rakesh's father, who came to work for me in the 1960s. I was used to living alone by then, having done so since my teens. But it was very quiet in the cottage (which was at the edge of a forest). The ghosts of long dead residents were sympathetic and unobtrusive and they kept to themselves. The song of the whistling thrush was beautiful, but I knew he was not singing for me. Up the valley came the sound of a flute sometimes, but I never saw the flute player.

It wasn't service that I needed but companionship. Prem, and then his wife and firstborn, little Rakesh, gave me that. They brought much love and laughter into my life. What more could a lonely man ask for?

It has been a long companionship. But it is the small things I remember. They come to me like pieces of cinema—coloured slides slipping across the screen of memory...

From the pine knoll across the valley, I see my cottage, Maplewood, washed by sunlight. Prem is in the garden, putting the mattresses out in the sun. From here he is just a speck on the far hill, but I know it is Prem by the way he moves slowly about the garden, pausing once in a while to look at the sky.

Prem rocking his infant son to sleep—crooning to him, passing his large hand gently over the child's curly head.

Prem following me down to the police station where I was arrested (for a story that appeared in *Debonair* magazine), and waiting outside until I reappeared.

Prem scolding Suzy the cat for the mess it had made.

Prem's large, irrepressible laughter, most in evidence when he was seeing an old Laurel and Hardy movie...

Most of my life I have given of myself, and in return I have received love in abundance. Life hasn't been a bed of roses. And yet, quite often, I've had roses out of season.

We must love someone.
We must keep loving, all our days,
Someone, anyone, anywhere
Outside our selves;
For even the sarus crane
Will grieve over its lost companion,
And the seal its mate.
Somewhere in life
There must be someone
To take your hand
And share the torrid day.
Without the touch of love
There is no life, and we must fade away.

I sit out in the open at night, after a shower of rain when the whole air is murmuring and tinkling with the voices of crickets and grasshoppers and little frogs. There is one melodious sound, a swift repeated trill, which I cannot place. Perhaps it is a tiny tree frog. Or it may be a small green cricket. I shall never know.

I'm not sure that I really want to know. In an age when a scientific and rational explanation has been given for almost everything we see, it is good to have a mystery, a mystery sweet and satisfying and entirely my own.

—

It's the simple things in life that keep us from going crazy. They contribute more to our general happiness and health than acts of passion and high excitement.

Like that pigeon in the skylight in the Delhi nursing home where I was incarcerated for two or three days. I was in a bad way, and even worse than the illness that had brought me there were the series of tests the doctors insisted I had to go through—ECGs, ultrasounds, endoscopies, X-rays, blood tests, probes into any orifice they could find, and at the end of it all a fat bill designed to give me a heart attack.

The only thing that prevented me from running into the street, shouting for help, was that pigeon in the skylight. It sheltered there at various times during the day, and its gentle cooing soothed my nerves. I owe my sanity to that pigeon.

And as I write this, I'm reminded of other consolations.

The winter sun on old bones.

The laughter of a child.

A cricket singing in a shady nook.

The smell of frying onions.

A small bird's nest.

A kiss in the dark.

New moon in a deep purple sky.

The day returns and brings us the petty round of irritating concerns and duties. Help us to play the man, help us to perform them with laughter and kind faces. Let cheerfulness abound with industry. Give us to go blithely on our business all this day, bring us to our resting-beds weary and content and undishonoured, and grant us in the end the gift of sleep.

—Robert Louis Stevenson

Sleep—'the gentlest of the gods', says Ovid. Cherish it. Honour it by giving it most of your night and an hour of your day when you can.

The evening drink, a good, light meal, a hot-water bottle in winter and an open window in summer—these are good sleeping aids, but none more important than a free and easy mind. 'With quiet mind go take thy rest,' said a wise man, and there is much truth in that statement. Forget and forgive at sunset, and then the day's deeds are truly done. Then sleep.

I think I have learnt something of the value of stillness. I don't fret so much; I laugh at myself more often; I don't laugh at others. I live life at my own pace. Like a banyan tree.

Is this wisdom, or is it just old age?

There is an old cane chair in the living room that has supported my considerable weight for well over thirty years. My wooden bed has done service for forty. My typewriter, too, which I used till it could no longer be repaired, did service for forty years. Since then I have relied on the pen and my fingers—which have served me quite well for at least seventy-five of my eighty years.

My books are old, most of my pictures are old; my shoes are old, my only suit is very old.

Only I am young.

Growing up was always a difficult process for me, and I gave up trying many years ago. I have the temper of a child, and a tendency to be mischievous. And I still retain a childlike trust in grown-ups, which sometimes works to my detriment. But it doesn't matter. In the long run, the exploiters and manipulators meet with their comeuppances; they are their own worst enemies.

Meanwhile, I'll continue being an eight-year-old. Recently, I was feeling a bit low, so I played marbles with the children. They won all my marbles, but I felt better.

—

I need some water, says the red geranium. Summer is just around the corner.

So, I water all the geraniums. And the nasturtiums. And the pea which is flaunting a little white flower at me.

The steps leading up from the road to our flat need repairing. But there are daisies growing in the cracks, so I shall let them finish flowering before doing anything about the steps.

—

A long and ne'er-say-die search for the perfect window. This would be one way to sum up my life. It began in my teens, and there were some rooms with passable views, but it wasn't until I moved into my present abode, a windswept, rather shaky old house on the edge of a spur, that I was truly satisfied. My bedroom window opens on to blue skies, mountains striding away into the far distance, winding rivers in the valley below (and, just to bring me down to earth, the local television tower).

The window is so positioned that I can lie on my bed and look at the sky, or sit at my desk and look at the hills, or stand at the window and look at the road below.

Which is the best of these views'?

Some would say the hills, but the hills never change. Some would say the road, because the road is full of change and movement—tinkers, tailors, tourists, salesmen, cars, trucks and motorcycles, mules, ponies and even, on one occasion, an elephant.

The road is never dull, but, given a choice, I'd opt for the sky. The sky is *never* the same. Even when it is cloudless, the sky colours are different. The morning sky, the daytime sky, the evening sky, the moonlit sky, the starry sky, these are all different skies. And there are almost always birds in the sky—eagles flying high, mountain swifts doing acrobatics, cheeky mynah birds meeting under the eaves of the roof, sparrows flitting in and out of the room at will. Sometimes a butterfly floats in on the breeze. And on summer nights, great moths enter at the open window, dazzled by my reading light. I have to catch them and put them out again, lest they injure themselves.

When the monsoon rains arrive, the window has to be closed, otherwise cloud and mist fill the room, and that isn't good for my books. But the sky is even more fascinating at this time of the year. From my desk I can, at this very moment, see the clouds advancing across the valley, rolling over the hills, ascending the next range. Raindrops patter against the window panes, closed until the rain stops.

And when the shower passes and the clouds open up, the heavens are a deeper, darker blue.

Darkness falls, and it is time to pull my chair to the window. Much that is lovely comes at this hour.

There is the fragrance of raat ki rani, queen of the night, from a neighbour's balcony, two feet by two. And soon there will be moonlight falling on those white flowers, and moonbeam in my room. Sometimes a field mouse drops in for a bite (he remembers my dinnertime). High in the treetops, an owl hoots softly, as if testing, trying to remember. The nightjar plays trombone, and the crickets join in to complete the orchestra. They go silent when the swamp deer calls. A leopard is out hunting.

A breeze has sprung up, it hums in the trees, and now the window is rattling. Time to shut the window. A star falls in the heavens.

Live close to nature and your spirit will not be easily broken, for you learn something of patience and resilience. You will not grow restless, and you will never feel lonely.

My relationship with the natural world has sustained and inspired me over the years. It is a relationship that has grown stronger and more meaningful ever since I came to live in the hills half a century ago.

'Is Nature your religion?' someone asked me recently. It would be presumptuous to say so. Nature doesn't promise you anything—an afterlife, rewards for good behaviour, protection from enemies, wealth, happiness, progeny, all the things that humans desire and pray for. No, Nature does not promise these things. Nature is a reward in itself. It is there, to be appreciated, to be understood, to be lived and loved. And in its way it gives us everything—the bounty and goodness of the earth, the sea, the sky. Food, water, the air we breathe. All the things we take for granted.

And sometimes, when we take it too much for granted, or misuse its generosity, Nature turns against us and unleashes forces that overwhelm us—earthquake, tidal wave, typhoon, flood, drought. But then it settles down again and resumes its generous ways.

For it is all about renewal—seasons and the weather, sunlight and darkness, the urgency of growth, the fertility of the seed and the egg. Governments rise and fall, machines rust away, great buildings crumble, but mountains still stand, rivers flow to the sea, and the earth is clothed with grass and verdure.

September 1994. Mussoorie had been under curfew for days. People had lost their lives at a rally for a separate state of Uttarakhand. The children's park on the Mall wore the look of a battlefield, and the fountain, dry for months, was splashed with blood. Violence of this nature was not something we had expected in our hill station. Our world had changed; after this tragedy perhaps it would never be the same again.

But there are compensations even during a curfew. Confined to the house, we must finally spend more time with our children; try to reassure them that the world is not such a bad place after all. Forage for food and make do with less of everything. Be friendlier with previously unsympathetic neighbours, because for once we are sharing the same hardships, the same uncertainty.

Since I lived outside the main bazaar and the hillside was just above me, I could safely defy the curfew and scramble up the slopes to discover anew the rich September flora. The wild ginger was in flower. So was agrimony, lady's lace, wild geranium. The ferns were turning yellow. The fruit of the snake lily had turned red, signifying an end to the rains. A thrush whistled on the branch of a dead walnut tree. A tiny swarm of butterflies rose from behind a lime-green bush.

When all the wars are done, a butterfly will still be beautiful.

Wars and upheavals destroy lives, but it is always worth remembering that life and humanity are bigger than them. We hear of heroic stands and superhuman perseverance, but fortitude and resilience are usually found in mundane things and are easily missed.

It was in Jersey, in UK's Channel Islands, that I first realized this. I was there for a year in the early 1950s. It was a quiet and very law-abiding island. Even through the German occupation during World War II, the islanders had gone about their business—mostly fishing and growing tomatoes—without paying much heed to the occupying power. And when the war ended in Europe, the Germans simply melted away and the islanders carried on growing their tomatoes. It was as though nothing had happened.

—

The smallest insect in the world is a sort of firefly and its body is only a fifth of a millimetre long. One can only just see it with the naked eye. Almost like a speck of dust, yet it has perfect little wings and little combs on its legs for preening itself.

That is perfection.

Walking along the beach as a little boy in Jamnagar, collecting seashells, I got into the habit of staring hard at the ground, a habit which has stayed with me all my life. Apart from helping my thought processes, it also results in my picking up odd objects—coins, keys, broken bangles, marbles, pens, bits of crockery, pretty stones, ladybirds, feathers, snail-shells. I use them to decorate my room, to make it more like the outdoors, full of little surprises.

Occasionally, of course, this habit results in my walking some way past my destination (if I happen to have one), and why not? It simply means discovering a new and different destination, sights and sounds that I might not have experienced had I ended my walk exactly where it was supposed to end. But I'm not looking at the ground all the time. Sensitive like the snake to approaching footfalls, I look up from time to time to examine the faces of passers-by, just in case they have something they wish to say to me.

A bird singing in a bush or tree has my immediate attention; so does any unfamiliar flower or plant, particularly if it grows in any unusual place such as a crack in a wall or a chimney, or in a yard full of junk, where I once found a rose-bush blooming on the roof of an old Ford car.

Slow down, and listen. There are sounds that are good to hear.

At night, rain drumming on the corrugated tin roof. It helps one to lie awake; at the same time, it doesn't keep one from sleeping. And it is a good sound to read by—the rain outside, the quiet within.

And early in the morning, when the rain has stopped, there are other sounds—a crow shaking the raindrops from his feathers and cawing rather disconsolately, but not sadly. Babblers and bulbuls bustling in and out of bushes and long grass in search of worms and insects. The sweet ascending trill of the Himalayan whistling thrush. Dogs rushing through damp undergrowth.

Some of the best sounds are made by water. The water of a mountain stream, always in a hurry, bubbling over rocks and chattering, 'I'm late, I'm late!' like the White Rabbit, tumbling over itself in its anxiety to reach the bottom of the hill. The sound of the sea, especially when it is far away—or when you hear it by putting a seashell to your ear.

Or the sound of a child drinking thirstily, the water running down her chin and throat.

Bullock-cart wheels creaking over rough country roads. The clip-clop of a tonga, and the tinkle of its bell.

Bells in the hills: A school bell ringing, and children's voices drifting through an open window. A temple bell heard faintly from across the valley. Heavy silver ankle bells on the feet of sturdy hill women. Sheep bells heard high up on the mountainside.

The sweet and solitary music of a flute at dusk.

A faraway voice on the shortwave radio, rising and fading through static.

—

The rich and famous have bought houses in this quiet part of our hill station. They come here for short visits and their big cars take over the winding roads.

Sometimes they invite their friends from the city and have jolly parties. The wind carries the muted sound of conversation, and the hillside rings with laughter. From a distance, these are good sounds on a cold and silent night. Theirs is not a party I would join, but the thought of happy people in the neighbourhood puts me in a good mood.

I am not, by nature, a gregarious person. Although I love people, and have often made friends with complete strangers, I am also a lover of solitude. Naturally, one thinks better when one is alone. I prefer walking alone to walking with others. That ladybird on the wild rose would escape my attention if I was engaged in a lively conversation with a companion. Not that the ladybird is going to change my life. But by acknowledging its presence, stopping to admire its beauty, I have paid obeisance to the natural scheme of things of which I am only a small part.

It is upon a person's power of holding fast to such undimmed beauty that his or her inner hopefulness depends. As we journey through the world, we will inevitably encounter meanness and selfishness. And as we fight for our survival, the higher visions and ideals often fade. It is then that we need ladybirds! Contemplating that tiny creature, or the flower on which it rests, gives one the hope—the certainty—that there is more to life than interest rates, dividends, market forces and infinite technology. There is space for the big and the small, for you and me and the ladybird.

Living in a small room for the greater part of my life, I have always felt the need for small, familiar objects that become a part of me, even if sometimes I forget to say hello to them. A glass paperweight, a laughing Buddha, an old horseshoe, a print of Hokusai's *Great Wave*, a suitcase that has seen better days, an old school tie (never worn), a potted fern, an old address book (not one address is relevant today, after some fifty years, but I keep it all the same).

Not all are objects. I had a pet tomato plant once, which did well in my sunny room. I have had geraniums in old cans. I had Suzie, a very independent-minded cat.

And today I remember the mouse who shared my little bed-sitting room in London when I was seventeen and all on my own. Those early months in London were lonely times for a shy young man going to work during the day and coming back to a cold, damp empty room late in the evening. In the morning I would make myself a hurried breakfast, and at night I'd make myself a cheese or ham sandwich. This was when I noticed the little mouse peeping at me from behind the books I had piled upon the floor, there being no bookshelf. I threw some crumbs in his direction, and he was soon making a meal of them and a piece of cheese. After that, he would present himself before me every evening, and the room was no longer as empty and lonely as when I had first moved in. He was a smart little mouse and sometimes he would speak to me—sharp little squeaks to remind me it was dinner time.

Months later, when I moved to another part of London, it was a fat little mouse I left behind.

—

Good company upon the road, says the proverb, is the
shortest cut.

—Oliver Goldsmith

Last night, as I lay sleepless
In the summer dark
With window open to invite a breeze,
Softly a firefly flew in
And circled round the room
Twinkling at me from floor or wall
Or ceiling, never long in one place
But lighting up little spaces...
A friendly presence, dispelling
The settled gloom of an unhappy day.

And after it had gone, I left
The window open, just in case
It should return.

I had wandered some way down the Tehri road, and it is quite late by the time I return to Landour Bazaar. Lights still twinkle on the hills, but the shopfronts are shuttered and the narrow street is silent. It is a cold night, doors and windows are shut. The people living on either side of the street can hear my footsteps, and I can hear the occasional loud remark, music from a transistor radio (this is before TV came to our hills), a burst of laughter, someone coughing and groaning in the dark.

A three-quarters moon is up, and the tin roofs of the bazaar, drenched with dew, glisten in the moonlight. The street is unlit, but I need no torch. I can see every step of the way. I can even read the headlines on the discarded newspaper lying in the gutter.

Although I am alone on the road, I am aware of the life pulsating around me. Three stray dogs are romping in the middle of the road. It is their road now, and they abandon themselves to a wild chase.

The rickshaw stand is deserted. One rickshaw catches the eye because it is decorated with marigolds, many of them still fresh.

A jackal slinks across the road, looking to right and left to make sure the dogs have gone. A field rat wriggles its way through a hole in a rotting plank, on its nightly foray among sacks of grain and pulses.

As I walk further along the empty street, under the shadow of the clock tower I find a boy huddled in a recess, a thin shawl wrapped around his shoulders. He is wide awake and shivering.

I pass by, head down, my thoughts already on the warmth of my room in the small cottage only a mile away. And then I stop. It is almost as though the bright moonlight has stopped me, holding my shadow in thrall. I make no conscious decision, but I'm walking back to the shadows where the boy crouches. He does not say anything, but he looks up at me, puzzled and apprehensive. All the warnings of well-wishers crowd in upon me—stories of crime by night, of assault, robbery, blackmail.

Well, we are equals, in our fear as in our loneliness.

I can tell from his features that he comes from the hills beyond Tehri. He has come here looking for work and he has yet to find any.

'Have you somewhere to stay?' I ask. He shakes his head; but something about my tone of voice has given him confidence, because now there is a glimmer of hope, a friendly appeal in his eyes.

I have committed myself. I cannot pass on. A shelter for the night—that's the very least one human should be able to expect from another.

'If you can walk some way,' I offer, 'I can give you a bed and blanket.'

He gets up immediately—a thin boy, wearing only a shirt and part of an old army tracksuit. He follows me without any hesitation. I cannot now betray his trust. Nor can I fail to trust him.

So now there are two in the sleeping moonlit bazaar. I glance up at the tall and shaky wooden houses, packed with families. They seem to lean towards each other for warmth and companionship.

The boy walks silently beside me. Soon we are out of the bazaar and on the footpath. The mountains loom over us. A fox crosses our path and a night-bird calls. And although no creature of the forest has ever harmed me, I'm glad I have a companion.

⌒

Geraniums are good companions. I can meditate upon a geranium. That is, I can spend a long time gazing at one. And as I can get geraniums to flower in my sunny bedroom, summer and winter, I have every opportunity to do so.

The geranium that has done best is the one I have grown in an old plastic bucket standing on the chest of drawers and facing the early morning sun. Here, protected from wind and rain, this generous plant has produced no less than eight florets of soft pink confetti. Other shades are appealing too—the salmon pink, the cerise, the flaming red—but this pale pink is restful, intimate. From my bed or desk I can gaze at it and have pleasant thoughts. Is that meditation? Or is it contemplation? The latter, probably. I am the contemplative type.

But meditation is in fashion—people give and take courses in it—whereas I have yet to meet someone taking a course in contemplation. I suspect that meditation is something that you do deliberately (hence the need for practice), and contemplation is simply what comes naturally.

When we meditate, we look within, and hopefully there is something to find there. When I look at a flower, I am looking without contemplating at the miracle of creation. I suppose we should do a little of both, just to get the right balance.

There are memories that we fear and run away from all our lives. But we also find solace in memory, often in unexpected ways, as unbidden images return from our past.

When I was living in London as a young man in the 1950s, I was homesick and miserable, separated by a thousand miles of ocean, plain and desert from my beloved Himalayas. And then one morning the depressing London fog became a mountain mist, and the sound of traffic became the *hoo-hoo-hoo* of the wind in the branches of tall deodar trees.

I remembered a little mountain path from my boyhood which led my restless feet into a cool forest of oak and rhododendron, and then on to the windswept crest of a naked hilltop. The hill was called Cloud's End. It commanded a view of the plains on one side, and of the snow peaks on the other. Little silver rivers twisted across the valley below, where the rice fields formed a patchwork of emerald green.

During the rains, clouds enveloped the valley but left the hill alone, an island in the sky. Wild sorrel grew among the rocks, and there were many flowers—convolvulus, clover, wild begonia, dandelion—sprinkling the hillside.

On the spur of the hill stood the ruins of an old brewery. The roof had long since disappeared and the rain had beaten the stone floors smooth and yellow. Some enterprising Englishman had spent a lifetime here making beer for his thirsty compatriots down in the plains. Now, moss and ferns grew from the walls. In a hollow beneath a flight of worn steps, a wildcat had made its home. It was a beautiful grey creature, black-striped, with pale green eyes. Sometimes it watched me from the steps or the wall, but it never came near.

No one lived on the hill, except occasionally a coal burner in a temporary grass-thatched hut. But villagers used the path, grazing their sheep and cattle on the grassy slopes. Each cow or sheep had a bell suspended from its neck, to let the shepherd boy know of its whereabouts. The boy could then lie in the sun and eat wild strawberries without fear of losing his animals.

I remembered some of the shepherd boys and girls.

There was a boy who played a flute. Its rough, sweet, straightforward notes travelled clearly across the mountain air. He would greet me with a nod of his head, without taking the flute from his lips. There was a girl who was nearly always cutting grass for fodder. She wore heavy bangles on her feet, and long silver earrings. She did not speak much either, but she always had a wide grin on her face when she met me on the path. She used to sing to herself, or to the sheep, or to the grass, or to the sickle in her hand.

And there was a boy who carried milk into town (a distance of about five miles), who would often fall into step with me. He had never been away from the hills. He had never been in a train. I told him about the cities (and why my hair wasn't black), and he told me about his village; how they made rotis from maize, how fish were to be caught in the mountain streams, how bears came to steal his father's pumpkins.

These things I remembered, crossing the street to a busy London tube station—these, and the smell of pine needles, the silver of oak leaves, the call of the Himalayan cuckoo, and the mist, like a wet facecloth. And as I stood in a crowded tube train between Goodge Street and Tottenham Court, my nose tucked into the back page of someone else's newspaper, I had a vision of a bear making off with a ripe pumpkin, and I had crossed a thousand miles of ocean, plain and desert and reached home.

Reading a book of Bhutanese wisdom, I came upon this little gem: 'Cold weather doesn't care if your coat is old or new.'

Given my sensual nature, I count myself lucky for having been spared the affliction of acquisitiveness. It is a matter of temperament; I was born this way, I can take no credit for it.

I began living on my own at seventeen. It was a tiny barsati in Dehradun. A bed, a table and a chair (by the window) were all that the room contained. It was all I needed—all that any writer needs. Even today, over sixty years later, my room contains the same basic furnishings—only the table is larger, to accommodate more in the way of paper and manuscripts; the bed is slightly more comfortable; and there is a rug on the floor. There's a separate room for my books—a luxury.

Yes, the rest of the house has grown, as my adopted family has grown. There is a television set in the dining room, a refrigerator in the kitchen. A few years ago we found we had saved enough to buy a car.

To be unconcerned about a desired good is probably the only way to possess it. To paraphrase Lao Tzu—one sure way to lose the world and everything in it, is to try grasping it.

Money often costs too much.

—Ralph Waldo Emerson

If you owe nothing, you are rich. Money doesn't make people happy.

But neither does poverty.

The secret, then, is to have as much as you need—or maybe a little more, and then share what you have.

'I enjoy life,' said Seneca, 'because I am ready to leave it.' If we can disencumber ourselves of nine-tenths of our worldly goods, it should not be difficult to leave the rest behind.

One of life's greatest pleasures is free. It lies in watching a plant grow—from seed to seedling, to green branch to bough, to flower to fruit.

As with many who love gardens, I have never really had enough space in which to create a proper garden of my own. The only time I had a patch of free earth at my disposal was back in the 1960s, when I was living in an old cottage on the outskirts of Mussoorie. Even then it was a few square feet of rocky hillside. All that I managed to grow on it were daisies—and they'd probably have grown there anyway. Still, they made for a charmingly dappled hillside throughout the summer, especially on full-moon nights when the flowers were at their most radiant.

For many years now, I have had to live in modest dwellings, sometimes on the upper floors of tumbledown buildings, which have no garden space at all. All the same, there are always a number of ever-widening cracks in which wild sorrels, dandelions, thorn apples and nettles—and sometimes a miniature peepul tree—all take root and thrive. You could call it a wild wall-garden, as pleasing a sight as any.

Let us cultivate our garden.

—Voltaire

I wouldn't go so far as to say that a garden is the answer to all our problems, but it's amazing how a little digging and friendly dialogue with the good earth can help reactivate us when we grow sluggish.

Before I moved into my present home, which has no space for a garden, I had, as I've said, a tiny patch on a hillside, where I grew some daisies. Whenever I was stuck in the middle of a story or an essay, I would go into my hillside garden and get down to the serious business of transplanting or weeding or pruning or just plucking off dead blooms, and in no time at all I was struck with a notion of how to proceed with the stalled story, reluctant essay, or unresolved poem.

Not all gardeners are writers, but you don't have to be a writer to benefit from the goodness of your gaindas and raat ki ranis. Baldev, who heads a large business corporation in Delhi, tells me that he wouldn't dream of going to his office unless he's spent at least half an hour in his garden. If you can start the day by looking at the dew on your antirrhinums, he tells me, you can face the stormiest of board meetings.

Or take Annie Powell, at one time my neighbour in Mussoorie, who at the age of ninety was up early every morning to water her little garden. Watering can in hand, she would move methodically from one flower bed to the next, devotedly giving each plant a sprinkling. She said she loved to see leaves and flowers sparkling with fresh water, it gave her a new lease of life every day.

———

Gardens remind me of one of the few friends I had as a child. His name was Dukhi and he took care of the garden in my grandmother's house in Dehradun. Time had no meaning in a large garden, and Dukhi never hurried. Life, for him, was not a matter of one year succeeding another, but of five seasons—winter, spring, hot weather, monsoon and autumn—arriving and departing. His seed beds had always to be in readiness for the coming season, and he did not look any further than the next monsoon. It was impossible to tell his age. He was either very young for his years or very old for them.

Dukhi loved bright colours, especially reds and yellows. He liked strongly scented flowers, like jasmine and honeysuckle. He couldn't understand my Granny's preference for the more delicately perfumed petunias and sweetpeas. But I shared Dukhi's fondness for the common bright orange marigold. When the garden was bare of all colour, the marigold would still be there, gay and flashy, challenging the sun.

Dukhi was very fond of making nosegays, and I liked to watch him at work. A sunflower formed the centre-piece. It was surrounded by roses, marigolds and oleander, fringed with green leaves, and bound together with silver thread. Was Dukhi really dukhi—sad? If he was, the garden kept him going.

There's a suitcase under my bed where I store old manuscripts and photographs, magazines and greeting cards from years ago that I couldn't throw away. It is a treasure I go to when I'm in need of diversion or comfort— the comfort of old friends, for memories can be friends. As, indeed, is the suitcase—still with me, sixty years after I bought it cheap as a homesick teenager in Jersey. It travelled back to India with me, and it has served me well. Like me, it's a bit battered but still functioning.

It isn't by throwing things away—and, invariably, replacing them—that we avoid cluttering up our life. It is by holding on to things that have been good and faithful to us. A trusted familiar knows how to live with us, finding its own space, giving us ours, and saves us from the need to hoard and possess that comes from feeling incomplete.

'Always tell the truth,' wrote Mark Twain, 'then you don't have to remember anything.'

I haven't always done that. So there's a truth. Most of us fail, and we always pay the price—with every lie we surrender a little of our peace of mind, because we never lie only once; a single lie births ten others. The trick, I suppose, is to make the effort to be truthful, for nothing liberates us like the truth. A life of simplicity is impossible without it.

And it is the same with forgiveness and letting go. We clutter up our life with grievances, hurts and regrets when we cannot forgive.

—

A local racketeer, who has been in jail a couple of times, meets me on the road and compliments me because I'm 'always smiling'. I think better of him for the observation.

Later that day I get a phone call from a lady who has sent me a slim volume of her poems, self-published. I tell her the poems are lovely.

If, by telling a lie, one can make someone happy, why not tell the damn lie?

A quiet sort of evening. I fix myself a rum and soda and settle down with one of my favourite books, *The Pocket Trivet: An Anthology for Optimists*, published by *The Morning Post* newspaper in 1932.

But what is a trivet, the unenlightened may ask. Well, it's a stand for a small pot or kettle, fixed securely over a grate. To be 'right as a trivet' is to be perfectly right—just right, like the short sayings in this book, which are further enlivened by a number of charming woodcuts based on seventeenth-century originals; such as the illustration of a moth hovering over a candle flame and below it the legend: 'I seeke mine owne hurt.' But the sayings are mostly of a cheering nature, such as Emerson's 'Hitch your wagon to a star!' Or the West Indian proverb: 'Every day no Christmas, an' every day no rainy day.'

My book of trivets is a happy example of much concentrated wisdom being collected in a small space—the beauty separated from the dross. It helps me to forget the dilapidated building in which I live and to look instead at the ever-changing cloud patterns from my bedroom window. There is no end to the shapes made by the clouds, or to the stories they set off in my head. We don't have to circle the world in order to find beauty and fulfilment.

After all, most of living has to happen in the mind. To quote one anonymous sage from my trivet: 'The world is only the size of each man's head.'

A thunderstorm, followed by strong winds, brought down the temperature. That was yesterday. And today it is cloudy, cool, drizzling a little, almost monsoon weather; but it is still too early for the real monsoon.

The birds are enjoying the cool weather. The green-backed tits cool their bottoms in the rainwater pool. A king-crow flashes past, winging through the air like an arrow. On the wing, it snaps up a hovering dragonfly. The mynahs fetch crow feathers to line their nests in the eaves of the house. I am lying so still on the window seat that a tit alights on the sill, within a few inches of my head. It snaps up a small dead moth before flying away.

At dusk I sit at the window and watch the trees and listen to the wind as it makes light conversation in the leafy tops of the maples. There is a whirr of wings as the king-crows fly into the trees to roost for the night. But for one large bat it is time to get busy, and he flits in and out of the trees. The sky is just light enough to enable me to see the bat and the outlines of the taller trees. Someone walks up the road below, whistling an old song.

There was something I had to do, but I think I will sit here a little longer.

When a small storeroom collapsed during the last heavy rains, I was forced to rescue a couple of old packing cases that had been left there for three or four years. The contents were well soaked and most of it had to be thrown away—old manuscripts that had been obliterated, negatives that had got stuck together, gramophone records that had taken on strange shapes (dear 'Ink Spots', how will I ever listen to you again?)... Unlike most writers, I have no compunction about throwing away work that hasn't quite come off, and I am sure there are a few critics who would prefer that I throw away the lot! Sentimental rubbish, no doubt. Well, we can't please everyone; and we can't preserve everything either. Time and the elements will take their toll. It is not a bad thing to be forced to travel light.

———

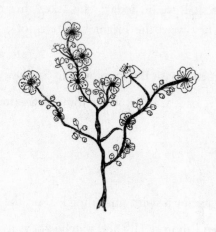

A memory from long ago. Ulla.

She woke fresh and frolicsome. The sun streamed in through the window, and she stood naked in its warmth, performing calisthenics. I busied myself with the breakfast. Ulla ate three eggs and a lot of bacon, and drank two cups of coffee.

'And what shall we do today?' she asked, her blue eyes shining. They were the bright blue eyes of a Siamese kitten.

'I'm supposed to visit the Employment Exchange,' I said.

'But that is bad. Can't you go tomorrow—after I have left?'

'If you like.'

'I like.'

And she gave me a swift, unsettling kiss on the lips.

We climbed Primrose Hill and watched boys flying kites. We lay in the sun and chewed blades of grass, and then we visited the Zoo, where Ulla fed the monkeys. She consumed innumerable ices. We lunched at a small Greek restaurant, and in the evening we walked all the way home through scruffy Camden Town, drank beer, ate a fine, greasy dinner of fish and chips, and went to bed early—Ulla had to catch a boat-train next morning.

'It has been a good day,' she said.

'I'd like to do it again tomorrow.'

'But I must go tomorrow.'

'But you must go.'

She turned her head on the pillow and looked wonderingly into my eyes, as though she were searching for something. I don't know if she found what she was looking for; but she smiled, and kissed me softly on the lips.

'Thanks for everything,' she said.

She was fresh and clean, like the earth after spring rain.

I took her fingers and kissed them, one by one. I kissed her breasts, her throat, her forehead; and, making her close her eyes, I kissed her eyelids.

We lay in each other's arms for a long time, savouring the warmth and texture of each other's bodies. Though we were both very young and inexperienced, we found ourselves imbued with a tender patience, as though there lay before us not just this one passing night, but all the nights of a lifetime, all eternity.

There was a great joy in our loving, and afterwards we fell asleep like two children who have been playing in the open all day.

The sun woke me next morning. I opened my eyes to see Ulla's slim, bare leg dangling over the side of the bed. I smiled at her painted toes. Her hair pressed against my face, and the sunshine fell on it, making each hair a strand of burnished gold.

The station and the train were crowded, and we held hands and grinned at each other, too shy to kiss.

'Goodbye,' she said. 'Give my love to Phuong.'

'I will.'

We made no promises—of writing, or of meeting again. Somehow our relationship seemed complete and whole, as though it had been destined to blossom for just those two days. A courting and a marriage and a living together had been compressed, perfectly, into one summer night...

I passed the day in a glow of happiness; I thought Ulla was still with me; and it was only at night, when I put my hand out for hers, and did not find it, that I knew she had gone.

But I kept the window open all through the summer, and the scent of the honeysuckle was with me every night.

Love is as mysterious as happiness—no telling when it may visit us; when it will look in at the door and walk on, or come in and decide to stay. I won't even hazard to say that love is always fleeting, a bird on the wing. I have known couples who grew old together and seemed reasonably happy.

There are few comforts greater than the touch of a loving hand when your hopes have been dashed. Of course things don't turn out that way for all of us. When I was young, I fell in love with someone, someone fell in love with me, and both loves were unrequited. But life carried on.

Nothing really ends happily ever after, but if you come to terms with your own isolation, then, paradoxically, it becomes immediately possible to find a friend. And friendship is also love.

A bat flies in through the open window. He flies very low, skimming the floor, zooming in and out under the single chair and table, seeming lost, as if his radar is wrong. I've grown quite used to him. And when sometimes he settles upside down at the foot of my bed, I let him be. On lonely nights, even a crazy bat is company.

—

It was March 1955 and I was returning to India, to everything I had missed keenly during my three years in the UK. Although I was twenty-one, and had been earning my own living for over three years, in many ways I was still a boy, with a boy's thoughts and dreams—dreams of romance and high adventure and good companionship. And I was still a lonely boy, alone on that big ship— passengers and crew all strangers to me—still sailing to an uncertain future.

I had two books with me—Thoreau's *Walden* and Richard Jefferies's *The Story of My Heart*—both reflecting my burgeoning interest in the natural world—but during the day the cabin was hot and stuffy, and the decks too crowded, so I postponed most of my reading until the journey was over. But at night, when it was cool on deck, and most of the passengers were down below, watching a film or drinking Polish vodka (it was a Polish ship), I would sit out under the stars while the ship ploughed on through the Red Sea. There was no sound but the dull thunder of the ship's screws and the faint tinkle of music from an open porthole.

And as I sat there, pondering on my future, a line from Thoreau kept running through my head. 'Why should I feel lonely? Is not our planet in the Milky Way?'

Wherever I went, the stars were there to keep me company. And I knew that as long as I responded, in both a physical and mystical way, to the natural world—sea, sun, earth, moon and stars—I would never feel lonely upon this planet.

A boy stretches out on the bench by the road like a cat, and the setting sun is trapped in his eyes, golden brown, glowing like a tiger's eyes. He reminds me of a friend from my youth; from long, long ago.

Where is he now? He would be an old man, like me. How much has he changed with time? How much have I?

I say a silent prayer for him and hope that he is happy and well. Because it makes me happy.

—

For as long as I can remember, I have been happiest taking a path—any old path will do—and following it until it leads me to a forest glade or village or stream or hilltop, or a face I long to see. But for some years now, I can rarely do this, and never on my own. Age demands the surrender of many pleasures (though they are replaced by other, less intense, more enduring ones).

So I turn to my diaries and notebooks to relive the days when I tramped all over my patch of the hills, sometimes sleeping at a roadside teashop or a village school.

Here's something I wrote of a winter afternoon some twenty years ago:

I have been cooped up in my room for several days, while outside it has rained and hailed and snowed and the wind has been blowing icily from all directions. It seems ages since I took a long walk. Fed up with it all, I pull up my overcoat, bang the door shut and set off up the hillside.

I keep to the main road, but because of the heavy snow there are no vehicles on it. Even as I walk, flurries of snow strike my face, and collect on my coat and head. Up at the top of the hill, the deodars are clothed in a mantle of white. It is fairyland: everything still and silent. The only movement is the circling of an eagle over the trees. I walk for an hour and pass only one person, the milkman on his way back to his village. His cans are crowned with snow. He looks a little high. He shakes my hand, gives me a tipsy salute, a tipsy grin and walks on, tipsily singing a Garhwali love song.

I come home exhilarated and immediately sit down beside the old stove to write. I find some lines of Stevenson's which seem appropriate:

> And this shall be for music when no one else is near,
> The fine song for singing, the rare song to hear!
> That only I remember, that only you admire,
> Of the broad road that stretches, and the roadside fire.

He speaks directly to me, across the mists of time: R.L. Stevenson, prince of essayists. There is none like him today. We hurry, hurry in a heat of hope—and who has time for roadside fires, except, perhaps, those who must work on the roads in all weathers?

Whenever I walk into the hills, I come across gangs of road workers breaking stones, cutting into the rocky hillsides, building retaining walls. I am not against more roads—especially in the hills, where the people have remained impoverished largely because of the inaccessibility of the villages. Besides, a new road is one more road for me to explore, and in the interests of progress I am prepared to put up with the dust raised by the occasional bus. And if it becomes too dusty, I can always leave the main road. There is no dearth of paths leading off into the valleys.

On one such diversionary walk, I reached a village where I was given a drink of curds and a meal of rice and beans. That is another of the attractions of tramping to nowhere in particular—the finding of somewhere in particular; the striking up of friendships; the discovery of new springs and waterfalls, rare flowers, strange birds.

And old familiars. Returning to Mussoorie from Rajpur around midnight, I saw a leopard leap over a parapet wall, then her three cubs scurrying into the bushes. I had thought I'd seen my last leopard some years ago. But there they were—a family of survivors.

I learned early—without quite realizing it—that the pleasure of travel is in the journey, and not so much in reaching one's destination. Destinations rarely live up to the traveller's expectations. And the pleasure is further reduced if you're checking your watch all the time. In travel, as in life, give yourself plenty of time, so that you won't have to rush—you miss seeing the world around you when you are in a great rush, or if you seal yourself off in air-conditioned cars and trains, afraid of the heat and dust.

I like to think that I invented the zigzag walk. Tiring of walking in straight lines, I took to going off at tangents— taking sudden unfamiliar turnings, wandering down narrow alleyways, following cart tracks or paths through fields instead of the main roads, and in general making the walk as long and leisurely as possible. In this way I saw much more than I would normally have seen. Here a temple, there a mosque; now an old church, now a railway line; here a pond full of buffaloes, there a peacock preening itself under a tamarind tree; and now I'm in a field of mustard, and soon I'm walking along a canal bank, and the canal leads me back into the town, and I follow the line of the mango trees until I am home.

The adventure is not in arriving, it's in the on-the-way experience. It is not in the expected; it's in the surprise. You are not choosing what you shall see in the world, but giving the world an even chance to see you.

It's like drawing lines from star to star in the night sky, not forgetting many dim, shy, out-of-the-way stars, which are full of possibilities. The first turning to the left, the next to the right... I am still on my zigzag way, pursuing the diagonal between reason and the heart.

—

Love your art, poor as it may be, which you have learned, and be content with it; and pass through the rest of life like one who has entrusted to the gods with his whole soul and all that he has, making yourself neither the tyrant nor the slave of any man.

–Marcus Aurelius

'Love your art, poor as it may be...' I have never regretted following this precept, despite the fact that it was sometimes difficult to make ends meet as a writer. The gift for putting together words and sentences to make stories or poems or essays has carried me through life with a certain serenity and inner harmony, which could not have come from any unloved vocation.

Within my own 'art' I think I have known my limitations and worked within them, thus sparing myself the bitter disappointment that comes to those whose ambitions stretch far beyond their talents. To know one's limitations and to do good work within them: more is achieved that way than by overreaching oneself. It is no use trying to write a masterpiece every year if you are so made as to write only one in ten or twenty. In between, there are other good things that can be written—smaller things, but satisfying in their own way.

Do what you know best, and do it well. Act impeccably. Everything will then fall into place.

I was looking for an example to try and illustrate this precept, and came upon it, some twenty years ago, in the persons of Mahboob Khan and Ramji Mal, stonemasons who were engaged in restoring Shah Jahan's Hall of Mirrors in the Agra Fort. They had been at work for nearly a decade, slowly but deftly bringing their epic task to completion.

The restoration work was so intricate that these two skilled craftsmen could restore only about six inches in a day. In recreating the original stucco work on walls and ceiling, everything had to be done impeccably; millions of pieces of tiny mirrors and coloured glass had to find their exact place in order to reflect just the right amount of light and, at the same time, conform to a certain pattern.

It was a small art, theirs, but it required infinite patience, skill and dedication. No fame for them, no great material reward. Their greatest reward came from the very act of taking pains in the pursuit of perfection.

Surely they must have been happy, or at least contented men. In truth, I have yet to meet a neurotic carpenter or stonemason or clay-worker or bangle-maker or master craftsman of any kind. Those who work with wood or stone or glass—those who fashion beautiful things with their hands—are usually well-balanced people. Working with the hands is in itself a therapy. Those of us who work with our minds—composers or artists or writers—

must try to emulate these craftsmen's methods, paying attention to every detail and working with loving care.

Because I have loved my art, I think I have been able to pass through life without being any man's slave or tyrant. I doubt I have ever written a story or essay or workaday article unless I have really wanted to write it. And in this way I have probably suffered materially, because I have never attempted a blockbuster of a novel, or a biography of a celebrity, or a soap opera. But in the end things have worked out well. I am a writer without regrets, and that is no small achievement!

There comes a time when almost every author asks himself what his effort and output really amount to. We expect our work to influence people, to affect a great many readers, when in fact its impact is infinitesimal. Those who work on a larger scale must feel discouraged by the world's indifference. That is why I am happy to give a little innocent pleasure to a handful of readers. This is a reward worth having.

As a writer, I have difficulty in doing justice to momentous events, the wars of nations, the politics of power; I am more at ease with the dew of the morning, the sensuous delights of the day, the silent blessings of the night, the joys and sorrows of children, the strivings of ordinary folk, and of course, the ridiculous situations in which we sometimes find ourselves.

We cannot prevent sorrow and pain and tragedy. And yet, when we look around us, we find that the majority of people are actually enjoying life! There are so many lovely things to see, there is so much to do, so much fun to be had, and so many charming and interesting people to meet... How can my pen ever run dry?

—

'Friendship, of itself a holy tie,' wrote Dryden. All my life has been the making of friends, and I have been luckier in this than most. I've been my own person, doing my own thing, and often stubborn. But, for the most part, I haven't lacked companionship. The trick, I think, is to trust people and not be suspicious of strangers—the people who become our friends are all strangers before they do.

The ancient Hebrew sage Hillel has been my guide:

> *If I am not for myself,*
> *Who will be for me?*
> *And if I am not for others,*
> *What am I?*
> *And if not now, when?*

'What's this?' asked Rakesh when he was a small boy, touching a huge horseshoe that stood on my desk.

'It's a horseshoe,' I said, 'I keep it for luck.'

And then I tell him them about Miss Bean, the old English lady who had grown up in Mussoorie, and who lived in Maplewood Cottage when I came to live there in 1963. The little cottage stood on its own on the edge of a maple and oak forest.

Miss Bean was in her eighties then, the 'last surviving Bean' as she described herself. Her parents, brother and sister were all buried in the Camel's Back Road cemetery. She received a tiny pension and lived in a small room full of bric-a-brac, bits of furniture rescued from her old home, and paintings done by her late mother. I was on my own then, living on sardines, baked beans, and other tinned stuff. Sometimes I shared my simple meals with her.

She told me stories of Mussoorie's early days—the balls and fancy dress parties at the Hackmans and Savoy hotels; the scandals that erupted from time to time; houses that were said to be haunted; friends who had gone away or gone to their maker; her father's military exploits.

I had noticed the big horseshoe on her mantelpiece, and asked her how she came by it. 'My father brought it over from England,' she said. 'It was supposed to bring us luck. But the good luck ran out long ago...You can have it, if you like it.' And she presented me with the horseshoe.

It has been with me for many years, going unnoticed most of the time, except when a visitor notices it and comments on its size.

Miss Bean passed away in her sleep, when I was still at Maplewood. Prem came to work for me soon after that and later brought his wife and three-month-old Rakesh from the village to live with us. They became my family. That was forty-three years ago.

Beena, Rakesh's wife, asked me one day, 'Did it really bring you good luck?'

'We make our own luck,' I said. 'But the horseshoe has been with us all these years, and it always reminds me of its former owner, a little old lady who didn't have much luck, but who enjoyed living, and stood alone, without complaining. It's courage, not luck, that takes us through to the end of the road.'

Miss Bean had the courage to stand alone. And she lives on through that old horseshoe on my desk.

By all means use sometimes to be alone!
Salute thyself: see what thy soul doth wear!

—George Herbert

It seems to me that most people are scared of solitude, for almost everything is carried out on a crowded scale. Clubs, wedding parties, sporting events, political meetings, victory parades, religious events, melas, even prayer meetings—the bigger the crowd, the more successful the event! Let a man be seen walking about the hills or countryside alone, and he will be labelled an eccentric.

For most people loneliness is wrongly linked to unhappiness. Their minds are not deep enough to appreciate the sweetness and balm of solitude; they are afraid of life itself, of coming face to face with themselves.

Most of the time we are taken up with family life or working for a living. To get away from it all, just once in a while, into the hills or fields or bylanes, where 'I am I', is to enjoy undisturbed serenity. It helps one to contemplate, to create a philosophy of life, to take the mind off the nagging cares of pressures of this age of technological mayhem.

But you do not have to turn your back on the world at large in order to find true solitude. A solitary spirit can move around with the crowd while still holding on to his innate reserve of solitude. Some people choose to sail around the world in small boats. Others remain in their own small patch, yet see the world in a grain of sand.

—

Homely sounds, though we don't often think about them, are the ones we miss most when they are gone. A kettle on the boil. A door that creaks on its hinges. Old sofa springs. Familiar voices lighting up the dark. Ducks quacking in the rain. Sounds that make a house a home.

—

One summer long ago, S___ came to stay with me in the cottage on the wooded hill. I would sometimes take the little path to the stream at the bottom of the hill, and now I did that with S___. I took her down to the stream and we walked some way downstream, holding hands to help each other over the rough rocks and slippery boulders. We discovered a little cavern, with little jets of water cascading down from above. There was an opening at the top, and a shaft of sunlight came through, mingling with the spray of water and creating a tiny rainbow. Yes, a rainbow! We had never seen anything like it.

Later, on our way back, we collected ferns. The shady places around Mussoorie harbour a variety of ferns, and we soon had more than we could handle. So we made a bed of ferns, and lay down upon them, and talked and touched each other and made promises which we wouldn't keep. Love is inconstant; but it was good to love. And it gave me memories that make me smile on gloomy days.

I see us now, S___ and I, younger, living in that moment and untroubled by the future, walking home like children, still excited about the little rainbow we had seen.

Another memory: On the road outside the cottage, someone came up to me in the dark and kissed me and ran away. Who could it have been? So soft and warm and all-encompassing...The moment stayed with me all night.

Who could it have been? I must find out. No, I must never find out.

There was light snowfall by morning. Just enough to cloak the deodars for an hour or two, before it all melted away.

—

Man cannot help but live in conformity with his nature; his subconscious is more powerful than his conscious mind.

A bright young schoolgirl once asked me, 'Sir, what is your philosophy of life?' She had me stumped. Should I tell her that I had just bumbled along? Would I disappoint her if I said that I was old but had no wisdom to offer? Well, better give her the truth, I decided, and had *her* stumped.

This morning I was pondering on this absence of a philosophy or religious outlook in my make-up, and feeling a little low because it was cloudy and dark outside, and gloomy weather always seems to dampen my spirits. Then the clouds broke up and the sun came out, large, yellow splashes of sunshine in my room and upon my desk, and almost immediately I felt an uplift of spirit. And at the same time I realized that no philosophy would be of any use to a person so susceptible to changes in light and shade, sunshine and shadow.

I am a pagan, pure and simple; sensitive to touch and colour and fragrance and odour and sounds of every description; a creature of instinct, of spontaneous attractions, given to illogical fancies and attachments. As a guide I am of little use to anyone, least of all to myself.

I think the best advice I ever had was contained in these lines from Shakespeare which my father had copied into one of my notebooks when I was nine years old:

This above all, to thine own self be true,
And it must follow as the night of the day,
Thou can'st not then be false to any man.

Each one of us is a mass of imperfections, and to be able to recognize and live with our imperfections—our basic natures, defects of genes and birth—makes, I think, for an easier transit on life's journey.

———

If you want something very badly, don't try too hard to seek it out, don't pursue it—better still, don't want it badly. You can generally get success if you don't want victory.

And it is not in mortals to *command* success.

———

The universe is full of magical things patiently waiting for our wits to grow sharper.

—Eden Phillpotts

Sometimes we are easily depressed by our surroundings, and it is rarely the case that we can change our surroundings. But we only need to look around us. The pebble at our feet, the wild flower growing out of rubble, dappled sunlight on an old wall—they have as much beauty as any work of art.

If a tiny room without a view is our fate, we can either resign ourselves to life in the cell, or do something to make it less dreary. I discovered that bare walls do nothing for the spirit, so I learnt to put pictures on them— photographs of friends or scenic places; even pictures of my favourite movie stars cut out from magazines.

Plants in old cans or bottles on the window sill. An oddly shaped stone as a paperweight. A comfortable chair, and a comfortable bed.

And then there's always the world outside. In my youth I stayed in cramped lodgings in the hot and dusty small towns of the Indian plains—perhaps the least inspiring places on earth—barely making a living by my writing. But long rambles in these towns surprised me with small miracles: moonlight on quiet alleys past midnight, for instance. Or the scent of quenched earth and fallen neem leaves after the first rains. Or the happy riot of the weekly bazaar. Or the brush of a stranger's hand that sometimes led to friendship and love.

Romance lurks in the most unlikely places.

A day without inspiration. My thoughts turn repeatedly to the mutton curry I've been promised for dinner. It will be a day of no achievement.

Should I feel guilty? That is hard work for me. I'd rather take a walk.

It is twilight. I walk to the top of the hill and watch the winter line. Successful day. And now I head back home for rum and Beena's mutton curry.

Some genuine early-monsoon rain, warm and humid, and not that cold high-altitude stuff we've been having all year. The plants seem to know it too, and the first cobra-lily rears its head from the ferns as I walk up to the bank and post office.

The monsoon season is one of the most beautiful times of the year in the Himalayas, with the mist trailing up the valleys, and the hill slopes a lush green, thick with ferns and wild flowers. The call of the kastura can be heard in every glen, while the barbet cries insistently from the treetops.

I wake up early after a night of thunder and rain and set out on a long walk because the sun is out. A great wild dahlia, its scarlet flowers drenched and heavy, sprawls over the hillside and an emerald-green grasshopper reclines on a petal, stretching its legs in the sunshine.

———

It was the first day of spring (according to the Hindu calendar), but here in the Himalayas it still seemed like mid-winter. A cold wind hummed and whistled through the pines, while dark rain clouds were swept along by the west wind only to be thrust back by the east wind.

I was climbing the steep road to my cottage when I was overtaken by nine-year-old Usha hurrying back from school. She had tied a scarf round her head to keep her hair from blowing. Dark hair and eyes, and pink cheeks, were all accentuated by the patches of snow still lying on the hillside.

'Look,' she said, pointing, 'a new flower!'

It was a single, butter-yellow blossom, and it stood out like a bright star against the drab winter grass. I hadn't seen anything like it before, and had no idea what its name might be. No doubt its existence was recorded in some botanical tome. But for me it was a new discovery.

'Shall I pick it for you?' asked Usha. 'No, don't,' I said. 'It may be the only one. If we break it, there may not be any more. Let's leave it there and see if it seeds.' We scrambled up the slope and examined the flower more closely. It was very delicate and soft-petalled, looking as though it might fall at any moment.

'It will be finished if it rains,' said Usha. And it did rain that night—rain mingled with sleet and hail. It rattled and swished on the tin roof; but in the morning the sun came out. I walked up the road without really expecting to see the flower again. And Usha had been right. The flower had disappeared in the storm. But two other buds, unnoticed by us the day before, had opened. It was as though two tiny stars had fallen to earth in the night.

—

The cosmos has all the genius of simplicity. The plant stands tall and erect; its foliage is uncomplicated; its inflorescences are bold, fresh, cheerful. Any flower, from a rose to a rhododendron, can be complicated. The cosmos is splendidly simple. No wonder it takes its name from the Greek cosmos, meaning the universe as an ordered whole—the sum total of experience. For this unpretentious flower does seem to sum it all up: perfection without apparent striving for it. Like the artistry of the South American footballer! Needless to say, it came from tropical America.

And growing it is no trouble. A handful of seeds thrown in a waste patch or on a grassy hill slope, and a few months later there they are, en masse, dancing in the sunshine. They are almost wild, but not quite. They need very little attention, but if you take them too much for granted they will go away the following year. Simple they may be, but not insensitive.

My respect for the cosmos goes back to my childhood when I wandered into what seemed like a forest of these flowers, all twice my height (I must have been five at the time) but looking down on me in the friendliest way, their fine feathery foliage giving off a faint aroma. Now when I find them flowering on the hillsides in mellow October sunshine, they are like old friends and I greet them accordingly, pressing my face to their petals.

Young couples, usually honeymooners, crowd the Mussoorie Mall. It is good to see new love in full bloom. Not all of them will remain in love with each other, but today they are and it makes them all beautiful, and fearless.

I have fallen in love many times. I *still* keep falling in love! As a youth, loneliness always went hand in hand with a powerful pull or attraction towards another person, be it boy or girl—and very often without that individual being aware of it. I think I expressed this feeling in a short poem, 'Passing By', which I wrote many years ego:

> *Enough for me that you are beautiful:*
> *Beauty possessed diminishes.*
> *Better a dream of love*
> *Than love's dream broken;*
> *Better a look exchanged*
> *Than love's word spoken.*
> *Enough for me that you walk past,*
> *A firefly flashing in the dark.*

It was probably written as a result of unrequited love. For whenever I pursued a loved one, that person proved elusive. On the other hand, the most lasting relationships have been those that have grown slowly, without fret or frenzy.

Declarations of passionate love or undying friendship are fine in their own way, and perhaps necessary; but the important thing is to feel comfortable with someone, and not have to keep proving yourself in one way or another.

In moments of rare intimacy two people are of one mind and one body, speaking only in thoughts, brilliantly aware of each other. I have known such moments—and who knows, I may know them again!

When things aren't going too well for me, I consult the *I Ching*, and usually get the right sort of wisdom and advice. Not so long ago, when I was suffering all the pangs of a rejected lover, I consulted the *Book of Change* and under the appropriate hexagram found the following lines:

'If you lose your horse, do not run after it,
It will come back of its own accord.'

In this case, it did not. But I made my peace with it. There's little point yearning after something that has been irredeemably lost. Of course, this is easier said than done. It is as hard to let go as it is to accept that something we long for intensely will never be ours. Some of us do it more successfully than others. I'm one of them. Lucky? I don't know. But I suppose I should be grateful.

I sit down to write. I finished a story yesterday, and that completed a book. So what should I begin today? There is a line of ants moving along the edge of the table and on to the wall. Well, then I shall record their resolute march.

The world may be in the grip of political and financial upheaval, but that does not mean the ants should stop going about their business. Their affairs are as serious as ours, and they make no noise about it.

'The Industrious Ant'. There, I have my title. This may grow into an essay, or it may become a poem, but I have begun, and that's half the job done.

I put down my pen, flex my fingers and lean back in my chair for a moment of rest, and the little rose begonia catches my eye. It has a glossy chocolate leaf, a pretty rose-pink flower, and it grows and flowers in my bedroom almost all the year round.

Some plants become friends. Most garden flowers are fair-weather friends; gone in the winter when times are difficult up here in the hills. Those who stand by us in adversity—plant or human—are our true friends; there aren't many around, so we must cherish them and take care of them in all seasons.

A loyal plant is the variegated ivy that has spread all over my bedroom wall. My small bedroom-cum-study gets plenty of light and sun, and when the windows are open, a cool breeze from the mountains floats in, rustling the leaves of the ivy. (This breeze can turn into a raging blizzard in winter—on one occasion, even blowing the roof away—but right now, it's just a zephyr, gentle and balmy.) Ivy plants seems to like my room, and this one, which I brought up from Dehradun, took an instant liking to my desk and walls, so that I now have difficulty keeping it from trailing over my notebooks when I am at work.

I like to take in other people's sick or discarded plants and nurse or cajole them back to health. This has given me a bit of a reputation as a plant doctor. Actually, all I do is give an ailing plant a quiet corner where it can rest and recuperate from whatever ails it—they have usually been ill-treated in some way. And it's wonderful how quickly a small tree or plant will recover if given a little encouragement. In return, there is gentle, generous friendship.

—

Loyalty in plants, as in friends, must be respected and rewarded. If dandelions show a tendency to do well on the steps of the house, then that is where they shall be encouraged to grow. If sorrel is happier on the window sill than on the hillside, then I shall let it stay, even if it means the window won't close properly. And if the hydrangea does better in my neighbour's garden than mine, then my neighbour shall be given the hydrangea. Among flower lovers, there must be no double standards. Generosity, not greed; sugar, not spite.

And what of the rewards for me, apart from the soothing effect of fresh fronds and leaves at my place of work and rest? Well, the other evening I came home to find my room vibrating to the full-throated chorus of several crickets who had found the ivy to their liking. I thought they would keep me up all night with their music; but when I switched the light off, they immediately fell silent.

Living for many years in Maplewood Cottage, at 7,000 feet in the Garhwal Himalayas, I was fortunate in having a number of trees surrounding me, giving me peace, security, the company of birds, and a variety of fruits for free.

Standing on its own was a walnut tree. In winter its branches were bare. In spring it would begin to come to life, each branch producing a hard bright spear of new leaf. By midsummer the entire tree was in leaf, and towards the end of the monsoon the walnuts, encased in their green jackets, had reached maturity.

Every year the tree gave me a basket of walnuts. But one year the walnuts were disappearing one by one, and I was at a loss to know who had been taking them. Could it have been the milkman's son? He was an inveterate tree climber. But he was usually to be found on oak trees, gathering fodder for his cows. He told me that his cows liked oak leaves but did not care for walnuts.

It wasn't the woodpecker. He was out there every day, knocking furiously against the bark of the tree, trying to prise an insect out of a narrow crack. He was strictly non-vegetarian.

One day I found a fat langur sitting on the walnut tree. I watched him for some time to see if he would help himself to the nuts, but he was only sunning himself. When he thought I wasn't looking, he came down and ate the geraniums; but he did not take any walnuts.

The walnuts had been disappearing early in the morning while I was still in bed. So one morning, I surprised everyone, including myself, by getting up before sunrise. I was just in time to catch the culprit climbing out of the walnut tree.

She was an old woman who sometimes came to cut grass on the hillside. Her face was as wrinkled as the walnuts she had been helping herself to. In spite of her age, her arms and legs were sturdy. When she saw me, she was as swift as a civet cat in getting out of the tree.

'And how many walnuts did you gather today, Grandmother?' I asked.

'Only two,' she said with a giggle, offering them to me on her open palm. I accepted one of them. Encouraged, she climbed back into the tree and helped herself to the remaining nuts. It was impossible to object. I was taken up in admiration of her agility in the tree. She must have been close to seventy, and I was forty-five, but I knew I would never be climbing trees again.

To the victor the spoils!

You stride through the long grass,
Pressing on over fallen pine needles,
Up the winding road to the mountain pass:
Small red ant, now crossing a sea
Of raindrops; your destiny
To carry home that single, slender
Cosmos seed,
Waving it like a banner in the sun.

I am in Dehra, many years after I lived there as a boy in my grandmother's house. I'm still young, thoughts of mortality are far from my mind, but there has been some struggle and sadness. Granny's house has been sold, it is out of bounds for me, but Dehra is still home.

In the cemetery there are several of my relatives; most of the rest have left for foreign shores. There are marigolds flowering at the edges of the graves. And a little blue everlasting that I have always associated with Dehra. It grows in ditches, on vacant plots, in neglected gardens, along footpaths, on the edges of fields, behind lime-kilns, wherever there is a bit of wasteland. Call it a weed if you like, but I have every respect for a plant that will survive the onslaught of brick, cement, petrol fumes, grazing cows and goats, heat and cold (for it flowers almost all the year round) and overflowing sewage. As long as that little flowering weed is still around, there is hope for both man and nature. There is hope for me.

I leave Dehra restored, hopeful, and by the time I have trekked halfway up Rajpur road, I'm hungry. A dhaba owner is busy at his tandoor and the smell of hot rotis draws me to the wooden bench outside his little establishment. A hot meal for less than two rupees and I'm ready to soldier on...

If a hundred per cent is not possible, let us attempt the ninety-five per cent that is.

In other words, we can't be perfect, but it is good to aim for perfection.

Which is never easy. It takes time, concentration, commitment, sacrifice. You have to give up things, certain pleasures, in order to give all your attention to the one thing that really matters—a cure for a disease, a scientific discovery, the near-perfect singing voice, mastery over a musical instrument, skill at a particular game, the completion of a literary masterpiece that people will actually read, the tilling of a field, the weaving of cloth.

In the effort lies the achievement; but only if the effort is true and made with all your heart.

—

Beer in the sun. High in the spruce tree the barbet calls, heralding summer. A few puffy clouds drift lazily over the mountains. Is this the great escape?

At some time during the day I must put pen to paper and produce something readable. There's not much money left in the bank.

Yes, but look at the honeybees—look at them push their way through the pursed lips of the antirrhinum and disappear completely. A few minutes later they stagger out again, bottoms first.

—

Fame is like the wind. It blows in all directions, then vanishes without warning. Not being a person of great eminence, I find myself encountering eminent people only when they are on the downslide to oblivion. People who have been in the limelight for a few years and then suddenly forgotten. Writers, actors, sportsmen, politicians—some hang on to fame a little longer than others, but most of us make our exits from the doors at which we entered. Once a star, and now taking a bit part. Once a major player, and now doing a commentary. Once an award-winning poet or novelist and now an alcoholic. Once a powerful leader, and now too old to be wanted at gatherings any more...

Time passes and brings us all down to the level of ordinary humans (which is where all of us belong). Some of us struggle and rant against the spectre of obscurity. I think we should welcome it. We have had our hour in the sun, and now we should come in from the glare and enjoy the shade.

Many words invite many defeats. The less a man knows, the longer he takes to tell it.

I am always a bit wary of saints and godmen, preachers and teachers, who are ready with solutions for all our problems. For one thing, they talk too much. When I was at school I mastered the art of sleeping (without appearing to sleep) through a long speech or lecture by the principal or visiting dignitary, and I must confess to doing the same today. The trick is to sleep with your eyes half closed; this gives the impression of concentrating very hard on what is being said, even though you might well be roaming happily in dreamland.

In our imperfect world there is far too much talk and not enough thought.

The TV channels are awash with gurus and experts telling us how to live, and they do so at great length. TV anchors are prone to lecturing and bullying the guests on their shows. Too many know-alls. A philosophy for living? You won't find it on your TV sets or in discourses by the loud lieutenants of the gods. You will learn more from your paan-wala or a street vendor.

'And what is your philosophy?' I asked my sabzi-wala.

'You have asked me this before, sir,' he said, as he chose a bunch of fresh greens for me.

'Yes, but what is your philosophy today?'

'The same as it was yesterday. Anything that helps me find a good customer.'

'My money will make you happy?'

'Only if my palak makes you happy and you come back for more,' he said and sent me on my way.

'Finish every day and be done with it,' wrote Emerson. 'You have done what you could. Some blunders and absurdities, no doubt, crept in. Forget them as soon as you can, tomorrow is a new day; begin it well and serenely, with too high a spirit to be cumbered with your old nonsense.'

But to get past our blunders, is it enough to forget? I'm not sure we can ever forget unless we remember, and accept that we were wrong.

We cannot undo what we have done, but we can earn a second chance.

—

Unpleasant experiences are best forgotten if one is not to become a bitter old cynic. But I was reminded of one recently, reading a memoir by the veteran journalist Vinod Mehta.

A story of mine that he had carried in *Debonair* magazine (of which he was the editor in the 1970s) had offended the guardians of our morals. The result was a criminal charge and I found myself under arrest.

No one who is under arrest is likely to enjoy the experience. Warrants make bad reading, except in detective stories. So how does a writer of modest prose and light verse take it? A nervous breakdown would not have been surprising, and did in fact seem likely. But I was saved from one by swallows.

There I was, sitting on a hard bench on the police station veranda, waiting for a couple of friends to arrive and stand bail for me, when I noticed the swallows wheeling in and out of the veranda, busily building a nest in the eaves of the old building. Nothing unusual about that. Swallows love old police stations. But just because it was so usual, so commonplace, I took heart.

The right word is *reassuring*. That is what we all need when we are in a tight corner—a little reassurance. Like a friendly, familiar face. Or the sleepy drone of a cricket commentary in the background. Or someone whistling cheerfully in a gloomy corridor. Something to let you know that even if things seem to be getting out of hand for a while, the rest of the world is still going on quite normally. And for me, nothing could have been more reassuring than the sight of several swallows—all oblivious to the terrors of the thana—going about their business.

Business as usual. That's what reassures. It bucked me up tremendously, just watching those little birds.

Presently an official came along, took me into his office, and asked me to fill a form. I said to him, 'Have you noticed that the swallows are nesting in the veranda?' He looked at me blankly. He hadn't noticed the swallows. What *were* swallows, anyway? Obviously I was deranged—a candidate for an asylum and not for jail.

But I knew then, watching the blank look on his face, that I was equal to the situation—that I was dealing with a human being whose plight was worse than mine, because he would never be able to find reassurance so quickly or so easily.

A night in the mountains:

It is the beginning of summer and I have trekked with a friend to his village in the Garhwal Himalayas. It has taken us a full day, and we are greeted outside the village by a buffalo herd wending its way homeward in the twilight, the gurgle of hookahs and the homely smell of cow-dung smoke.

And after an evening with friends over rum, and a partridge for dinner, we retire to our beds: I to my charpai under a lime tree at the edge of the courtyard. The moon had not yet risen and the cicadas are silent.

I stretch myself out on the charpai under a sky tremendous with stars. And as I close my eyes someone brushes against the lime tree, bruising its leaves, and the good fresh fragrance of lime comes to me on the night air, making the moment memorable for all time.

—

A morning in the mountains:

I wake to the sound of a loud cicada in the lime tree near my bed. It is just after first light, and through the pattern of the leaves I see the outlines of the mighty Himalayas as they stride away into an immensity of sky. I can see the small house, where I am a guest, standing in the middle of its narrow terraced fields. I can see the other houses, standing a little apart from each other in their own bits of land. I can see trees and bushes, and a path leading up the hill to the deodar forest on the summit.

The tops of the distant mountains suddenly light up as the sun torches the snow peaks. A door bangs open. The house is stirring. A cock belatedly welcomes the daylight and elsewhere in the village dogs are barking. A magpie flies with a whirring sound as it crosses the courtyard and then glides downhill. And suddenly everyone, everything comes to life, and the village is buzzing with activity.

Trekking in the Himalayan foothills back when I could do that, I once walked for kilometres without encountering habitation. I was just scolding myself for not having brought along a water bottle when I came across a patch of green on a rock face. I parted a curtain of tender maidenhair fern and discovered a tiny spring issuing from the rock—nectar for the thirsty traveller.

I stayed there for hours, watching the water descend, drop by drop, into a tiny casement in the rocks. Each drop reflected creation. That same spring, I later discovered, joined other springs to form a swift, tumbling stream, which went cascading down the hill into other streams until, in the plains, it became part of a river. And that river flowed into another mightier river that kilometres later emptied into the ocean.

Be like water, taught Lao-Tzu, philosopher and founder of Taoism. Soft and limpid, it finds its way through, over or under any obstacle, sometimes travelling underground for great distances before emerging into the open. It does not quarrel; it simply moves on.

—

The whistling thrush is here again, bathing in the rainwater puddle beneath the window. He loves this spot. So now, when there is no rain, I fill the puddle with water, just so that my favourite bird keeps coming.

His bath finished, he perches on a branch of the walnut tree. His glossy blue-black wings glitter in the sunshine. At any moment he will start singing.

Here he goes! He tries out the tune, whistling to himself, and then, confident of the notes, sends his thrilling voice far over the forest.

———

Late March. End of winter.

The blackest cloud I've ever seen squatted over Mussoorie, and then it hailed marbles for half an hour. Nothing like a hailstorm to clear the sky. Even as I write, I see a rainbow forming.

—

The rain stops and my friend departs. I wish he had stayed, I wish the rain had not stopped so soon.

But then the clouds begin to break up, and the sun strikes the hill on my left. A woman is chopping up sticks. I hear the tinkle of cowbells. Water drips from a leaking drainpipe. And suddenly, clear and pure, the song of the whistling thrush emerges like a dark sweet secret from the depths of the ravine.

—

A smart young journalist came up to interview me on the occasion of my eightieth birthday, and the release of a new book. (Whether it was the former that was more newsworthy or the latter, I don't know!) 'You are eighty and yet you are so active and continue to write. What is the secret of your energy?' he asked.

'The secret,' I told him, 'is to give in to my lazy nature. Sleep when I want to, eat when I want to, read a lot of books and sit on old walls, dreaming.'

Sitting on walls, apparently doing nothing, has always been my favourite form of inactivity. But for these walls, and the many idle hours I've spent upon them, I would not have written even a fraction of the stories, essays and other diversions that I have. It is not the walls themselves that set me off or give me ideas, but a personal view of the world that I receive from sitting there.

Creative idleness, you could call it. A receptivity to the world around me—the breeze, the warmth of the old stone, the lizard on the rock, a raindrop on a blade of grass—these and other impressions impinge upon me as I sit in that passive, benign condition that makes people smile tolerantly at me as they pass. 'Eccentric writer,' they remark to each other, as they drive on, hurrying towards the pot of gold at the end of their personal rainbows. I wave to them as they rush off, and wish them luck.

Sitting inside Mussoorie's Cambridge Bookshop on a rainy day, watching the world pass by, signing books or pieces of paper for the occasional reader (it is off season), I am reminded of E.M. Forster. Not Forster himself, but his immortal line of exactly two words: 'Only connect.'

As in life, so in art: only connect. I have always believed that to communicate and be readable is all that a writer should aim for. People ask me why my style is so simple. I think it is because I want my readers to feel what I feel, to see what I see, and big words and big sentences get in the way of this sharing. It is clarity and honesty that I am striving to attain; there can be no lasting connection with my readers without these. And to be clear and open is to be simple.

The heart of the matter is never complicated. Nor do we need too many words to get to it and share it. My theory of writing is that the conception should be as clear as possible, and that words should flow like a stream of clear water. You will, of course, encounter boulders, but you will learn to go over them or around them, so that your flow is unimpeded. If your stream gets too sluggish or muddy, it is better to put aside that particular piece of writing. Go to the source, go to the spring, where the water is purest, your thoughts as clear as the mountain air; where there is no struggle.

Of course some people *want* literature to be difficult. And there are writers who like to make their readers toil and sweat. Perhaps they hope to be taken more seriously that way. Well, that is not my way, but I wish them loyal readers, too!

And as I write this, I think of my father. Long before I began thinking seriously about words and sentences, and the art of simplicity, he gave me advice on communication. It was in the last letter he wrote me:

'I wanted to write before about your writing, Ruskin, but forgot. Sometimes I get letters from you written in very small handwriting, as if you wanted to squeeze a lot of news into one sheet of letter paper. I know your handwriting is good and that you came first in class for handwriting, but try and form a larger style of writing and do not worry if you can't get all your news into one sheet of paper—but stick to big letters.'

It was my first lesson in clarity.

'Writing is easy,' said Red Smith. 'All you have to do is sit at your typewriter till little drops of blood appear on your forehead.' That's true for some of us. But I refuse to suffer. At the first sign of drops of blood or perspiration, I get up from my desk and do something totally different—make myself a sandwich, water my ferns, take a walk or discuss politics and the weather with the milkman. If the writing isn't easy, if I'm not enjoying it, I know I'm better off doing something else.

And yet writing is easy if I'm happy with my theme. Ask me to write a piece on petunias and I'll turn out an enthusiastic essay on this underrated flower. I might even write a story on someone who grows petunias, because such a person must obviously have sterling qualities. And I might delve into the love life of a petunia grower because those who love flowers must, by their very nature, be loving, even sensual and passionate people. But ask me to write the life story of a political leader or media tycoon and I'm stumped and stymied. Those little drops of blood threaten to appear. I cannot breathe life into these subjects, noble though they might be. Their true personalities, the essence of their natures, somehow elude me. It is not that they are too complicated, but rather that one has to peel off too many layers of protective armour to get at the flesh and blood that lies beneath the skin. The big words delivered for effect, the careful poses, the smooth manner in which they can say one thing and mean quite another—or nothing at all—prevent us from coming anywhere close to the heart and mind of our hero.

I am most at home in small places—Shamli and Saharanpur; Darjeeling and Dehra; Karnal and Kasauli; Meerut and Mussoorie....These are the places I know best, and where I have found my friends and heroes, and my stories.

I think Tolstoy summed it all up when he said: 'One ought only to write when one leaves a piece of one's flesh in the ink-pot each time one dips one's pen.'

To which I might humbly add: There is something to be said for ink-pots. And the hand that holds the pen. It must be far more difficult to share one's body and soul with a typewriter or computer. I abandoned the typewriter long ago. There is something intimate about writing by hand. It takes me back to my childhood, when I was first learning to write letters and join them together. When I had any difficulty, my father would put his hand on mine and guide it along the page.

His hand is still there. I feel it now, even as I write.

And may loving, long-gone hands touch yours, dear reader.

We are not alone.

Quarrelled with R___, and later felt foolish and made up. When will I learn that life is not a novel? Life does not have the organization of a novel. People are not characters in a play; they refuse to conform to the exigencies of a plot, or our desires, or even our needs.

We have to accept people as they are if we want to live with them. We can't really change people. Only a chameleon can change colour, and then only in order to deceive us.

You cannot take the love but spurn the lover.

—

We age without really knowing that it's happening.

I got up one morning, sat on the edge of my bed, went into a reverie, and ten minutes later, found I was still sitting on the edge of my bed. And I was the goalkeeper of my school football team! When did I become so old?

Later that day, I thought I would take a walk. I climbed down the steps from the flat, and immediately sat on the parapet wall on the road to rest.

Professor Uniyal rode up on his scooter, stopped and remarked, 'Mr Bond, I recognized you from behind!'

'Well, thank you, kind sir,' I said, 'better to be recognized from behind than never to be recognized at all.'

A sense of humour will help you get through the worst of times!

I wish to be a Taoist. I'm old and still trying. But here's a page from a journal I kept in my thirties:

'A mighty storm last night. It was as if the entire hillside would be carried away by the terrible wind. Prem is happy, laughing, giggling all the time. Sometimes it is a little annoying for me, because he is obviously unaware of what is happening around him—such as the fact that part of the roof blew away in the storm—but I am a good Taoist, I say nothing, I wait for the right moment! Besides, it is a crime to interfere with anyone's happiness.'

Who says we get better with age?

Cervantes: 'God bless the inventor of sleep, the clock that covers all men's thoughts.'

Cervantes got it right. He usually did. The siesta was of course invented in Spain, before it was exported to Mexico and the rest of the world. Here, in India, it was something of a necessity. The perspiring farmer takes an afternoon nap beneath a banyan tree. The bania pulls down the shutters of his shop, if only for an hour's slumber. The busy executive switches on the air-conditioning and is unavailable because of a 'meeting'.

I have my meetings too, usually at night, or at dawn, when the sweetest of dreams come to me and make me long to sleep again. My afternoon siestas are not dreamy, they are made up of solid sleep, and woe betide the intruder who awakens me. My language is then at its most colourful.

Why do I sleep so soundly and so peacefully, at any time of the day or night? Some say it's because of a clear conscience. But my conscience is not clear. I am full of guilt. Is sleep the clock that covers my guilt?

Or is it age? Or is it simply because I have a soft pillow? A pillow can make all the difference to one's life. Sleep with the wrong pillow and you'll wake up an angry man. The right pillow, and you wake up a happy man.

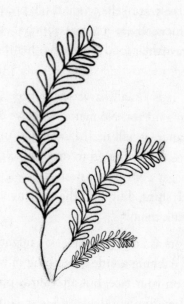

A restaurant in town has acquired a brand new look. The walls are now covered with tall mirrors. Wherever the diners turn, they see their reflection. Most of them stare in fascination and often forget their food. Few look happy, the rest are self-conscious. I preferred the old wooden panels. Everyone was much better company then, and gave their food and each other their undivided attention.

I find that it is usually a waste of time gazing at our reflection in a mirror. No matter what we do to improve our appearance, it will be the same old unexciting face that will look back at us from one day to the next. And we will only get a one-dimensional view—a face to launch a thousand ships, but not the sagging backside that helped to sink them!

Avoid mirrors as far as possible. You might need one for shaving, or dabbing a little something of whatever must be dabbed on your face, but afterwards put it away and try looking at the world instead—the contours are far more interesting.

A wild species of geranium (the round-leaved crane's bill, to give its English name) with a tiny lilac flower has responded to my overtures, making a great display in a tub where I encouraged it to spread. Never one to spurn a gesture of friendship, I have given it the freedom of the shady back veranda. Let it be my flower of the month, this rainy August.

I don't think I could have got through life without the company of flowers. They sustain and stimulate. My desk is just a place of work until Beena or one of the children places a vase of flowers upon it, and then it becomes a place of delight. Be it a rose or a chrysanthemum or a simple daisy, it will help me in my work. The flowers are there to remind me that life has its beautiful moments.

My preference, though, is for wild flowers. Most things that will not be tamed are more appealing than those that are eager to please. When I step out for one of my walks, I look for wild flowers, even the most humble of flowers hiding on the hillside. And if don't know their names, I invent their names, because it's nice to know someone by his or her name.

An amateur botanist I know is dismissive of the names I have invented. 'The correct name,' he begins in his learned, unbending manner—and then he utters many complex and unpronounceable scientific words. Is it any surprise that flower enthusiasts like me blunder when it comes to distinguishing types and families of flowers?

Botanists have done their best to intimidate and confuse the nature lover. But we should not allow ourselves to be discouraged; we have as much right to the enjoyment of wild flowers as they.

So I will disregard the botanist and I will go looking for the pretty flower that I have named Merry Heart. It is always nodding and dancing in the breeze. It is a happy flower, deserving of a happy, light name.

There's beauty in the sight of things, in the sound of things. And, in the clear air of the mountains, there's beauty in the smell of things.

I like the smell of certain leaves, even more than the scent of flowers. Crushed geranium and chrysanthemum leaves, mint and myrtle, lime and neem trees after rain, and the leaves of ginger, marigolds and nasturtiums, and fallen pine needles.

When I lie on summer grass in some Himalayan meadow, I am conscious of the many good smells around me—the grass itself, redolent of the morning's dew, bruised clover, wild violets, tiny buttercups and golden stars and strawberry flowers and many others I shall never know the names of (which makes the fragrance sweeter).

And the earth itself. It smells different in different places. But its loveliest fragrance is known only when it receives a shower of rain. And then the scent of the wet earth rises as though it would give something beautiful back to the clouds. A blend of all the fragrant things that grow upon it.

I remember an aunt who sometimes came to stay with my grandmother, and who had an obsession about watering the flowers. She would be at it morning and evening, an old and rather lopsided watering can in her frail hands. To everyone's amazement, she would water the garden in all weathers, even during the rains.

'But it's just been raining, Aunt,' I would remonstrate. 'Why are you watering the garden?'

'The rain comes from above,' she would reply. 'This is from me. They expect me at this time.'

—

In a month of fluctuating moods, some of the things I have enjoyed:

Three bright orange nasturtiums taking the sun at my window.

Two women, seen from a distance, chattering and laughing under a walnut tree.

Tuning in at random to a BBC request programme and hearing Nelson Eddy sing 'Rose Marie'.

Watching little Shrishti grow quite pretty.

Getting a cheque in the mail.

—

We shall not spoil what we have by desiring what we have not, but remember that what we have too was the gift of fortune.

—Epicurus

Epicurus gave us the word epicurean, denoting a love of the good things in life, and presumably he enjoyed the best of all possible worlds, or else he would not be so uncomplaining.

Good fortune is usually passed on to us by our forebears, who have made fortunes by dint of hard work and by 'desiring what they have not'; and so Epicurus, dear man, was talking a lot of rubbish.

To be born in a hovel is not the gift of fortune; to grow up hungry is not the gift of the gods. It is only by desiring what we have not, and striving for it, that we have any chance of sharing in that good fortune which may have been 'gifted' to the lucky few.

What we should worry about is not desiring what we have not, but desiring too much, and desiring only for ourselves.

Holi brings warmer days, ladybirds, new friends. And trees in new leaf.

I love the pine, but my guide is the hospitable deodar tree. It allows other things to grow beneath it, and it tolerates growth upon its trunk and branches—moss, ferns, small plants.

I may not have contributed anything towards the progress of civilization, but neither have I robbed the world of anything. Not one tree or bush or bird or flower. Even the spider on my wall is welcome to his space.

—

I'm watching the stars from my window. Every time I see the sky I am aware of belonging to the universe rather than to just one corner of the earth.

And in the silence that settles in the hills at night, the smallest sounds become clear—a field mouse rustling through dry leaves, a seed falling, and the drip of the dew running off the roof.

If I am lucky, I see the moon coming up silently over the far mountains.

There are moments that come to each of us, moments when we feel deeply moved or inspired, when time seems to stand still and we become acutely aware of the benediction of sun and wind and trees. Then heaven is here, compensating for the irritations and disasters that we build around ourselves each day.

And heaven seems to turn up when we least expect it. Many years ago, I gave up a good job in Delhi and came to live in the Mussoorie hills, partly because I love mountains and forests, partly because I wanted to devote more time to writing, and partly because I knew, instinctively, that I would find companionships here that would endure. I lived at the edge of a forest of oak and maple. I was happy among trees but the full magic of a tree was only brought home to me some years later, when I was visiting the plains.

I was walking through a stretch of wasteland, a desert that seemed to stretch endlessly across a wide, flat plain. Just as I was beginning to find the heat and the glare a little discouraging, I saw a tree, just one small, crooked tree shimmering in the distance. And seeing it there all by itself, but growing stubbornly where other trees would not grow, I was filled with love and admiration for it. When I reached the tree, I found that it had given shelter to other small plants from the sun. A pair of parrots emerged from a hole in the tree trunk and flew across the plain, flashes of red and green. Finding that tree there, struggling on its own but giving life to other things, was like finding a bit of heaven where I least expected it.

Almost always, it's the unexpected that delights us, that takes us by the throat and gives us a good shaking, leaving us gaping in wonder. It may only be a shaft of sunlight slanting through the pillars of a banyan tree or dewdrops caught in a spider's web or, in the stillness of the mountains, clear, sweet birdsong or the sudden chatter of a mountain stream as one rounds the bend of a hill.

These little miracles don't happen especially for us. Sunlight will filter through leaves, dew will settle on a spider's web, birds will sing and a mountain stream bubble and chatter even when there is no one around to see or hear. All that is in our power is to be there. To be there, wherever we are.

The wind in the pines and deodars hums and moans, but in the chestnut it rustles and chatters and makes cheerful conversation. The horse chestnut in full leaf is a magnificent sight.

If you have the ability, or rather the gift, of being able to see beauty in small things, then old age should hold no terrors.

I do not have to climb a mountain peak in order to appreciate the grandeur of this earth. There are wild dandelions flowering on the patch of wasteland just outside my windows. A wild rose bush will come to life in the spring rain, and on summer nights the honeysuckle will send its fragrance through the open windows.

I do not have to climb the Eiffel Tower to see a city spread out before me. Every night I see the lights of the Doon twinkling in the valley below; each night is a festive occasion.

I do not have to travel to the coast to see the ocean. A little way down the Tehri road there is a tiny spring, just a freshet of cool, clear water. Further down the hill it joins a small stream, and this stream, gathering momentum, joins forces with another stream, and together they plunge down the mountain and become a small river and this river becomes a bigger river, until it joins the Ganga, and the Ganga, singing its own song, wanders about the plains of India, attracting other rivers to it bosom, until it finally enters the sea. So this is where the ocean, or part of it began. At that little spring in the mountain.

I do not have to take passage to the moon to experience the moonlight. On full-moon nights, the moon pours through my windows, throwing my books and papers and desk into relief, caressing me as I lie there, bathing in its glow. I do not have to search for the moon. The moon seeks me out.

All this, and more, is precious, and we do not wish to lose any of it. As long as our faculties are intact, we do not want to give up everything and everyone we love. The presentiment of death is what makes life so appealing; and I can only echo the sentiments of the poet Ralph Hodgson:

> *Time, you old gypsy man,*
> *Will you not stay,*
> *Put up your caravan*
> *Just for one day?*

N_{ight.}

Glow-worms shine fitfully in the dark. The night is full of sounds—the tonk-tonk of a nightjar, the cry of a barking-deer, the shuffling of porcupines, the soft flip-flop of moths beating against the windowpanes. On the hill across the valley, lights flicker in the small village—the dim lights of kerosene lamps swinging in the dark; there has been no power since the afternoon's storm.

The full moon rides high, shining through the tall oak trees near the window. And floating across the valley from your village, my lost friend, the sound of drums, beating. I hope I dream of you tonight. I may have stopped loving you, but I will never stop loving the days I loved you.

Sometimes it is hard to believe that I've been up here in the hills all these years—fifty summers and monsoons and winters and Himalayan springs (there is no real spring in the plains)—because when I look back to the time of my first coming here, it seems like yesterday.

That probably sums it all up. Time passes, and yet it doesn't pass; people come and go, the mountains remain. Mountains are permanent things. They are stubborn, they refuse to move. You can blast holes out of them for their mineral wealth; or strip them of their trees and foliage, or dam their streams and divert their currents; or make tunnels and roads and bridges; but no matter how hard they try, humans cannot actually get rid of the mountains. That's what I like about them; they are here to stay.

I like to think that I have become a part of this mountain, this particular range, and that by living here for so long, I am able to claim a relationship with the trees, wild flowers, even the rocks that are an integral part of it. Yesterday, at twilight, when I passed beneath a canopy of oak leaves, I felt that I was a part of the forest. I put out my hand and touched the bark of an old tree, and as I turned away, its leaves brushed against my face, as if to acknowledge me.

The beginning of spring. The sun pouring into my room brings with it a delicious warmth. My bones, muscles, arteries, nerves, all feel relaxed, such a relief after three months of wincing from the cold. A girl from Kerala drops in for a chat, bringing with her all the warmth of the South.

Outside, small trees and shrubs are in new leaf; tiny flowers appear on the retaining walls and here and there there's a touch of green; butterflies appear from nowhere. A mynah bird alights on the window sill, delivers a short speech, waits for me to nod my approval and takes off.

Spring is the time of life renewed, the mynah said. The time of a green and reviving earth, of nesting and mating and birth. Of hope.

Hope! Yes, it is the season of hope—the season when, like the unfurling leaf, we are reaching for something beyond ourselves.

It is spring and the sap is rising.

I feel it too, old as I am. I would like nothing better than to hold someone warm and beautiful in my arms, once again. Am I asking for too much? Well, one can always dream... No one can take our dreams away!

And until death comes, all is life.

Bright red
The poinsettia flames,
As autumn and the old year wanes.

ABOUT THE AUTHOR

Ruskin Bond was born in Kasauli in 1934, and grew up in Jamnagar, Dehradun, Delhi and Shimla. He is the author of over a hundred books, among them: his autobiography, *Lone Fox Dancing*; the novellas *The Room on the Roof* and *A Flight of Pigeons*; the short story collections *The Night Train at Deoli*, *Time Stops at Shamli* and *Our Trees Still Grow in Dehra*; and the non-fiction books *Rain in the Mountains* and *Landour Days*. He received the John Llewellyn Rhys Prize in 1956, the Sahitya Akademi Award in 1993, the Padma Shri in 1999 and the Padma Bhushan in 2014. He lives in Landour, Mussoorie with his adopted family.

Ruskin
Bond
LONE FOX DANCING
• My Autobiography •